The Our Father

by Fr Andrea Gasparino

All booklets are published thanks to the generous support of the members of the Catholic Truth Society

CATHOLIC TRUTH SOCIETY
PUBLISHERS TO THE HOLY SEE

Contents

Introduction 3

Our Father Who Art In Heaven 7

Hallowed Be Thy Name 13

Thy Kingdom Come 19

Thy Will be Done on Earth as it is in Heaven 27

Give us this Day Our Daily Bread 35

Forgive us our Trespasses 45

Lead us not into Temptation 53

Deliver us from Evil 57

Introduction

In giving us the Our Father, Jesus gave us a way to pray. The Our Father is not so much a prayer that is complete in itself, more a way of praying, a pattern for prayer; it is not so much a 'ready-made' prayer, more a prayer requiring further development; it is not so much a prayer that needs to 'be said'; but more a prayer that needs to 'be done'. It is a kind of route map to pray with.

The Our Father is much more then than a mere formula to be recited. To get the best out of it, we need to ponder it clause by clause and get right inside it, for we will find there a whole programme for our lives.

The two versions of the Our Father

We have two versions of the Our Father. Biblical experts tell us that Luke's version appears to be the older one, while the version contained in Matthew perhaps represents a partial rewording of Luke's original... Here are the two versions:

Luke 11:2-4
Father,
Hallowed be your name,
your kingdom come;
give us each day our daily bread,
and forgive us our sins,
for we ourselves forgive each one
who is in debt to us.
And lead us not into temptation.

Matthew 6:9-13
Our father in heaven,
hallowed be your name,
your kingdom come,
your will be done,
on earth as it is in heaven.
Give us today our daily bread.
And forgive our debts,
as we have remitted the debts
of those who are in debt to us.
And do not lead us into temptation,
but deliver us from the Evil One.

In teaching us the Our Father, Jesus shows himself an incomparable teacher of freedom who fully respects our capacity for initiative: rather than putting words into our mouths, he gives us ideas that we can develop in our own words.

The Our Father was the disciples' own special prayer, it was like a membership badge. It was in fact given by Jesus in response to a specific request by the disciples: 'teach us to pray, as John taught his disciples.' (*Luke* 11:1) It is for this reason that the Church gives it solemnly to the baptised person. It is our baptismal prayer.

A harmoniously-structured design

It will be helpful to begin by taking a bird's-eye view of the route we are going to follow together. The ideas in the Our Father follow a harmoniously-structured design which it is important for us to grasp.

After first addressing God as 'Our Father', we come before him with three commitments and three requests:

1. A commitment to bear witness: 'Hallowed be your name';

2. A commitment to faithfulness: 'Your kingdom come';

3. A commitment to love: 'Your will be done';

4. A request for God's support: 'Give us this day our bread';

5. A request for forgiveness of sins: 'Forgive us our debts';

6. A request for salvation from evil: 'Do not lead us into temptation, but deliver us from evil'.

First Jesus invites us to give and then he invites us to ask; first we commit to being the kind of people God wants us to be, then we ask for what we need to provide for our material and spiritual necessities. And so the Our Father becomes a sublime 'prayer that needs to be done'.

The purpose of what follows will be to offer a sober spiritual commentary on each individual clause that makes up the Our Father.

Our Father Who Art In Heaven

The word 'Father' as addressed to God was not exclusive to the Jews but was used by many ancient peoples.

In India the word 'father' was used to designate the sky and the word 'mother' to designate the earth - i.e. the two principles that give their origin to the universe.

The Sumerian peoples of Mesopotamia (the first known people to use writing) possessed a hymn to the lunar God 'Sin' in which they called God 'Compassionate Father'.

In Greek and Roman civilisation Zeus, Jupiter, was often called 'father of the gods and men'. The philosopher Plato used the name 'father' for the idea of good, the supreme reality.

The Jews applied the name 'Father' to God in Scripture in a metaphorical sense, and we find it fifteen times in the Old Testament. Here are some of the texts:

'Is this not your father, who gave you being, who made you, by whom you subsist?' (*Deuteronomy* 32:6)
'you are our Father; we are the clay and you are our potter, all of us are the work of your hands'.
(*Isaiah* 64:7)

'For I am a father to Israel'. (*Jeremiah* 31:9)

'As tenderly as a father treats his children, so Yahweh treats those who fear him'. (*Psalms* 103:13)

'for Yahweh reproves those he loves, as a father the child whom he loves.' (*The Proverbs* 3:12)

'Lord, father and master of my life'. (*Ecclesiasticus* 23:1)

In the New Testament the word 'Father' appears 170 times, and it was Jesus who brought down to earth the true notion of God as Father. While the Jews always used the word 'father' in a metaphorical sense, Jesus went far beyond this; for it is virtually certain that when Jesus spoke of God as 'Father' he used the Aramaic term Abbà, the word a child uses to address its daddy.

On Gethsemane Jesus prayed: 'Abbà... for you everything is possible. Take this cup away from me.'

(*Mark* 14:36). This has to be an expression that Jesus used habitually, otherwise Mark would not have used it at such a solemn and tragic moment. To apply this word to God was scandalous for the Jews, but Jesus used it.

Paul and John: 'we are sons'

Paul exhorts us to use this word too, and he gives us the reason why: 'As you are sons, God has sent into our hearts the Spirit of his son crying, 'Abba, Father'; and so you are no longer a slave, but a son'. (*Galatians* 4:6-7)

In the Letter to the Romans too he repeats: 'for what you received was not the spirit of slavery to bring you back into fear; you received the Spirit of adoption, enabling us to cry out, 'Abba, Father!' (*Romans* 8:15)

By virtue of our connection with Jesus we are true children of God, and so we have the right to call God 'Father'. It is no longer a metaphor, it is a reality: God's closeness to us through Jesus overrides blood ties.

St John too repeated to the first Christians: 'You must see what great love the Father has lavished on us by letting us be called God's children - which is what we are!' (*1 John* 3:1)

'Our' Father: praying in the plural

Jesus teaches us to pray in the plural. Not one invocation in the Our Father is in the singular, not even the request for the forgiveness of sins. This means that Jesus understands prayer not just as a lifting up of our hearts to God, but also as a profound opening-up to our brothers.

'Each one of us should feel that we are in a filial relationship with God. But this 'vertical' awareness is not to be separated from the 'horizontal' one of our union in the Spirit with all our fellows' (*Troadec*).

'When we say 'Our Father' we not only mean to say that we are praying with Christ, but that we are praying in Him with all those who live in him, with all humanity present and past, because in him death does not matter any more. We are also praying with Mary, with Peter, with Paul, with Francis, with Dominic, with Ignatius, we are praying with all our loved ones who are no more, who have now been born again in Christ' (*Peter Calvay, hermit*).

The word 'our' is quite sufficient by itself to create the context of all prayer. Prayer should help us to go out of ourselves, it should take us gradually into Christ's world, and through him into the world of our fellows, the world of all of humanity.

Father, 'who art in heaven'

The Jews believed that there were several heavens and that God lived in the inaccessible part of them (see *Psalm* 104). The expression 'who art in heaven' underlines the transcendence of God, his infinite greatness.

There is a stark and profound contrast between the expression 'Father', which speaks of intimacy and closeness, and the words that follow it - 'who art in heaven', which speak of transcendence and of the infinite. One expression complements the other. Why is God Father to us, why is he intimate with us - because He is the Infinite one, the Transcendent one.

When the Muslim prays he invariably expresses his veneration of the transcendence of God, but Jesus teaches us that it is not enough to be dazzled by God's transcendence, we must allow his goodness and his closeness to us, soften our hardness.

'Father' and 'who art in heaven', two ideas that are almost contradictory, become complementary in the prayer of Jesus. They mean: 'Father, you who are the Infinite one (i.e. the omnipotent one, the omnipresent one, the transcendent one), but to us you are Father, and we are all one with you'.

Hallowed Be Thy Name

To a Semite the name always designates the person in the depth of his being. Thus, for a Semite, to utter the name of a person makes him present.

In Isaiah 43:1, God says: 'I have called you by your name' This clearly means 'I have known you to your depths'.

In Psalm 20:8 the expression: 'Some call on chariots, some on horses, but we on the name of Yahweh our God' means 'we have faith in the person of the Lord, in his power'.

In John 17:6 Jesus says: 'I have revealed your name to those whom you took from the world to give me' means 'I have made known your person, your love'.

When Jesus changes Peter's name he says: 'You are Cephas/Peter and on this rock I will build my Church.' (*Matthew* 16:18)

So in the Jewish world the name has a very great significance, it provides a focus and an expression for a person's characteristics.

To hallow is a Semitic term. It can have two meanings:

1. To consecrate a profane thing to God, to treat a profane thing as holy. It is in this sense that in Exodus 20:8 we are told to 'hallow the sabbath' i.e. make it sacred to God;

2. Or it has the meaning of reverencing, of giving respect and trust.

It is used in this sense in Ezekiel 36:23, where God says: 'I am going to display the holiness of my great name, which has been profaned among the nations... And the nations will know that I am Yaweh' which means: 'I will make my person be reverenced'.

In the New Testament it is used in this way too. In 1 Peter 3:15 we find the words 'proclaim the Lord Christ holy' with the meaning of 'revering' or 'adoring' the divinity of Christ.

'Hallowed be your name' therefore signifies: 'may respect, veneration, trust be given to your person'.

Respect, veneration, trust

When we pray, Jesus wants us first and foremost to ask for respect, veneration, and trust in God. Here are five different possible ways of understanding this:

1. *Father, above all purify the knowledge that men have of you!*

There is colossal ignorance about God in the world, even in those of us who consider ourselves Christians. In reality our idea of God is often steeped in childishness, superstition, and fear. Christ does not tolerate ignorance about God, and we need to purify our faith of all that disfigures the truth about God that Jesus has given to us.

In a heartfelt prayer, Jesus spoke these words: 'And eternal life is this: to know you... and Jesus Christ whom you have sent.' (*John* 17:3) Our salvation depends on the knowledge that we have of God! We are responsible for all our mental profanations of God, for all our ignorance, and indeed ignorance about God sounds the death-knell of our faith!

A second way of reading the words 'hallowed be your name' runs like this:

2. *Father, let me not profane you in myself, may you occupy the right place in my life, the first place!*

Far from being at the heart and centre of our lives, God is all too often just one more among many things. God is often nothing more than a vague reality that is very far from touching our existence to its depths. Jesus teaches us that this problem must be close to our hearts more than any other problem, and he calls us to put praying about it at the top of our list of priorities.

The way we Christians dishonour God with our absenteeism is one of our weightiest responsibilities. Nietzsche said: 'Show me you are redeemed and I will believe in your Redeemer'.

3. *Father, hallowed be your name, may I not profane you, may you not be misrepresented through my fault.*

My life and my behaviour mirror my religious convictions. A pagan life proclaims openly that God is nothing to me, a Christian life proclaims that God matters a great deal to me, a saintly life proclaims that God is truly everything to me.

4. *Father, hallowed be your name, may you be loved through my love.*

Our generosity in giving ourselves to our brothers brings God to those brothers. Through our love our fellows will come to understand the power of the love of God.

5. *Father, hallowed be your name, send down plenty of saints to earth!*

We are to ask God to send saints down among us, for saints are signs of the inner progress of a people, saints make God visible on earth.

The world needs saints more than anything, so we have to ask God for them. We must keep asking for saints, we must ask for a whole host of saints.

Holy priests: for the world of the young desperately needs holy priests.

Holy fathers and mothers: for there are too many pagan parents; our parishes need holy spouses to raise the next generation.

Holy professionals, holy doctors, holy workers: for it is only through saints that God gains access to hostile environments.

Young saints: youth needs a great rash of holiness.

Thy Kingdom Come

*E*xperts consider this to be the heart of the Our Father. It is the key sentence in the prayer of Christ, for all the message of the gospel of Christ is centred on this theme - the coming of the Kingdom and the urgency of entering the Kingdom. It is a constant topic in the gospels, where Matthew refers to the Kingdom 49 times, Mark 16 times, and Luke 38 times.

What is the Kingdom?

The Gospels do not present a political or a territorial picture of the Kingdom. Everyone knows what Jesus said to Pilate: 'Mine is not a kingdom of this world' (*John* 18:36). The gospels present the kingdom of God as something spiritual.

Mark reports the first preaching of Jesus like this: 'The time is fulfilled, and the kingdom of God is close at hand. Repent and believe in the gospel.'

(*Mark* 1:15). If the Kingdom that is coming requires an inner conversion, and this means that the words 'Kingdom of God' are to be understood first as God taking possession of human hearts. From another text it appears that the Kingdom of God is the victory over Satan: 'But if it is through the finger of God that I drive devils out, then the kingdom of God has indeed caught you unawares.' (*Luke* 11:20)

There is no extant definition of the Kingdom, though Jesus did give a description of it in a very rich series of parables. Here are some of them:

- the parable of the darnel implies that the Kingdom is the struggle for good which is always opposed by evil - but the final victory will be God's;

- the parable of the mustard seed tells us that the Kingdom is the good growing on earth like a plant, at first insignificant, then impressive;

- the parable of the leaven tells us that the Kingdom is a mysterious force that pervades humanity and that will make it ferment for God;

- the parable of the hidden treasure and the precious pearl tells us that the Kingdom is the supreme value for us, above which we are not to rate anything else, and for which it it is right to stake everything;

- the parable of the fishing-net presents the Kingdom as a challenge of God to the world to gather in (to fish) all men of good will;

- the parable of the dinner guest presents the Kingdom as a great feast at God's table that is open to all, and that includes even the most wretched.

The coupling of parallel phrases

To determine the meaning of 'Kingdom of God' more precisely, it will be helpful to study the exploitation of parallel phrasing in the Our Father.

Parallelism is a literary artifice typical of oriental poetry, where it is used in a similar way to rhyme. It is extremely helpful for exegetes, because we can very often determine the meaning of a sentence by studying the parallel sentence with which it is coupled. For example, in Psalm 121:5 we find: 'Yahweh is your guardian, your shade/Yahweh at your right hand'.

The second part almost always explains, amplifies or clarifies the first. A careful study of the the Our Father reveals that it is composed of four parallel clauses coupled together.

First parallelism
Our Father who art in heaven (who reign in the universe)/hallowed be your name (may it reign in us).

Second parallelism
May your kingdom come/may your will be done.

Third parallelism
Give us this day our daily bread (material good)/forgive us our sins (spiritual good).

Fourth parallelism
Lead us not into temptation/but deliver us from evil.

A careful study of one half of each of the parallel clauses in the couplings sheds light on the other. So if we ask what is meant by 'Your Kingdom come', the answer is almost certainly that it means 'your will be done'. In other circumstances in fact Jesus said: 'It is not anyone who says to me, "Lord, Lord," who will enter the kingdom of heaven.' (*Matthew* 7:21).

From all that has been said so far we can conclude that the Kingdom is:

A big family
gathered around the Father in heaven,
made up of persons of good will,
saved by God,
Devoted to good,
who fight against evil,
ready to do the will of God in a perfect manner
as it is fulfilled in heaven.

There is a slow relentless battle for good that will last up to the end of the world. It is for this reason that the prayer 'Your Kingdom come' ought to be constantly on our lips, since our participation in the Kingdom will always be under threat right up to the final definitive establishment of the eternal Kingdom of God.

'Thy Kingdom come'

Why did Jesus invite us to ask for the coming of the Kingdom? Evidently because he wants us to desire it with all our hearts, simply because it is our greatest good to desire to fulfil the will of God with absolute faithfulness.

'Thy Kingdom come' is therefore a personal commitment to follow the will of the Father as perfectly as possible.

'Thy Kingdom come' means that we assent personally to entering into the joy of friendship with God. In fact Jesus also presents the Kingdom as a feast, a festive banquet at God's table, but he admonishes us to observe the strict laws of hospitality (the wedding garment, see *Matthew* 22:11).

'Thy Kingdom come' means being converted, i.e. 'changing one's mentality' (metánoia): 'Repent, the Kingdom of God is close at hand.' (*Mark* 1:15).

'Thy Kingdom come' means reminding ourselves and God that hard daily battle awaits us if we are to carry out the will of the Father faithfully. We really have to prepare ourselves for it.

'Thy Kingdom come' means accepting the principle of the beatitudes, it means trusting in God rather than in our own strength.

'Thy Kingdom come' means accepting our own limitations, it means becoming like children, sincere, pure, trusting; it means always choosing the truth in all things. '...Unless you change and become like little children you will never enter the kingdom of Heaven.' (*Matthew* 18:3).

'Thy Kingdom come' means accepting that there will be struggles, misunderstandings in the cause of right, and even persecution: 'Blessed are those who are persecuted in the cause of uprightness: the kingdom of Heaven is theirs.' (*Matthew* 5:10)

'Thy Kingdom come' means courageously choosing the way of charity and forgiveness. God forgives, but man, despite being forgiven so much by Him, often refuses to forgive.

'Thy Kingdom come' means choosing detachment from consumerism and a comfortable 'middle-class' existence: 'it is easier for a camel to pass through the eye of a needle than for someone rich to enter the kingdom of Heaven.' (*Matthew* 19:24).

'Thy Kingdom come' means a complete break with evil. The Kingdom is actually Christ's victory over Satan: '...if it is through the Spirit of God that I drive out devils, then be sure that the kingdom of God has caught you unawares.' (*Matthew* 12:28).

There can be no possible compromise between Christ and evil. Christ expects us to make a choice: 'Anyone who is not with me is against me, and anyone who does not gather in with me scatters.' (*Matthew* 12:30).

Thy Will be Done on Earth as it is in Heaven

In the Our Father the focus is always on God, and this is a general rule of prayer, for we all too often fall into the trap of focusing our prayers on ourselves.

A whole programme of life, perfect and complete in extension and profundity, can be found in this small portion of the Our Father.

To begin with we need to get a good grasp of the words. The Greek text was translated as 'may your will be done', but instead of 'done' the original is 'become'. In other words, the petition asks that the will of God 'may come', 'become', or 'go forward'. The will of God is presented as something that is fulfilled independently of us, and yet, as in the case of the Kingdom, we are invited to play our own part, no matter how small.

The words are easy enough to make sense of, but there are hidden depths in them that call for further reflection. Jesus is inviting us to ask for two things:

1. For a desire to give our assent to the will of God;

2. For a desire to give our complete assent ('on earth as it is in heaven').

Why does Jesus want us to ask for this? The truth is that doing the will of God is not a simple matter, since his will is often the opposite of our own, and we are far more inclined to follow our own will than his. Moreover, to give complete assent to his will is almost impossible for us in our weakness without God's help.

Levels of generosity

There is a whole range of levels of generosity in the way we assent to the will of God, and the degree of generosity in our assent mirrors the degree of our openness to him.

There is a resentful kind of acceptance, when we say 'yes' to God but reluctantly. The truth is that this is refusal rather than assent, since it is forced. People often react like this when they are deeply traumatised by a heart-breaking bereavement. But this may be a first instinctive reaction and perhaps not fully conscious.

Then there is a resigned assent, an assent that is incomplete. Our weakness often conditions the way that we react to deeply traumatic events.

Then there is real assent which corresponds to a high level of love for God. It can be given even in the heart of the deepest darkness, as with the assent of Jesus in Gethsemane. It may represent a truly heroic step for a particular individual, a step that simply cannot be taken without the help of God.

Then there is full self-abandonment into God's hands. This is a step forward, this is love, faith, and hope. It is the act by which a person ceases to argue with God and embraces God's plans in faith.

Finally there is an active collaboration with the will of God: here we get down to the nitty-gritty, we have to leave behind our own cherished purposes and make a full and responsible decision to embrace the will of God with all our strength.

This way of complete assent to the will of God is far from easy for us, and Jesus is all too aware of this, for he puts this human problem at the heart of the prayer to the Father. In so doing, he puts it at the heart of all his teaching.

Assent to the will of God is the focus of all Christ's spirituality: 'My food is to do the will of the one who sent me' (*John* 4:34). 'I seek to do not my own will but the will of him who sent me.' (*John* 5:30). 'My Father... Let it be as you, not I, would have it.' (*Matthew* 26:39).

Moreover, assent to the will of the Father is at the heart of all Christ's teaching about following him: 'It is not anyone who says to me "Lord, Lord," who will enter the kingdom of Heaven, but the person who does the will of my Father in heaven.' (*Matthew* 7:21). 'Anyone who does the will of my Father in heaven is my brother and sister and mother.' (*Matthew* 12:50).

So it was that Paul wrote to the first Christians: 'So be very careful about the sort of lives you lead, like intelligent and not like senseless people... This is why you must not be thoughtless but must recognise what is the will of the Lord.' (*Ephesians* 5:15, 17).

How to determine the will of God

It is not sufficient simply to conform to the will of God, for Jesus goes even further, he asks us to do the will of God perfectly: 'Thy will be done on earth as it is in heaven'. In other words in a divine manner - or in essence, the way Jesus did it himself.

Such depth can make us giddy, and it raises an immediate problem: how to determine the will of God? This is far from easy for us. There are three ways: one of them is very clear, the other two are more uncertain and difficult.

1. *The first way is 'The word of God'*. This is an open road, and it is always within our reach. Jesus made this way even simpler, he smoothed it out some more by making it clearer. He focused all that he expects from us and all that he commands us into one single point: charity. 'This is my commandment: love one another, as I have loved you.' (*John* 15:12). 'It is by your love for one another that everyone will recognise you as my disciples' (*John* 13:35).

2. *The second way of discerning the will of God is by reading the signs contained in events* - especially all those events that are outside any possible control by us.

There are so many of them! Life, death, health, intelligence, gifts and weaknesses, success and failure, friendships and enmities. Then there are the wider events by which we are conditioned, even when we don't want to be: the social, cultural, and political contexts of our lives, peace, war, the climate, catastrophes. These are all events that lie mainly outside our control: all we can do is live them and suffer them.

They are tunnels through which we must pass with courage and faith, accepting what our conscience tells us to accept as willed by God.

3. The third way of discerning the will of God is more difficult: it is the fulfilment of our duties. Sometimes our duty is simple and clear, even if it is never easy to follow perfectly. Sometimes it leaves us perplexed:

   - is it my duty to speak? Is it my duty to be silent?

   - Is it my duty to intervene? Up to what point? On what issue?

   - Is it my duty to prevent? To encourage? How far?

- Is it my duty to tell someone off? Is it my duty not to do so?

Difficulties often multiply and increase our perplexity, but God cannot be far from any person of good will.

Living the asceticism of the present moment

If someone asks 'is there some simple way for me to move forward here and now in my daily life in faithfulness to the will of God? The answer is that there is a very simple tactic which is within the capacity of all persons of good will: it is what some authors call the asceticism of the present moment.

The only moment that we possess is the present moment. The minute just past is no longer mine, the minute that is just coming is not yet mine. I am terribly but happily anchored to the situation of the present moment. I can live this situation in total presence or else I can leap over it, running away into the past or the future, i.e. denying to the present moment the devotion with which I ought to be living it.

The asceticism of the present moment can be said to go back to Jesus when he taught: 'So do not worry about tomorrow: tomorrow will take care of itself. Each day has enough trouble of its own.' (*Matthew* 6:34).

It could be said that to live the present moment well is the great motorway of sanctity for the weak and poor person, for the person who distrusts his strength. To do extraordinary things it is often necessary that we be extraordinary people, but to do our duty well moment by moment, not many things are needed. All we need is a bit of will-power and a bit of love.

This is the life of heroism for the person who does not feel like a hero, it is the way of peace for the person who is for ever anxious, it is the way of faith.

Give Us This Day Our Daily Bread

The first three clauses of the Our Father had to do with the interests of God, the three that now follow have to do with the interests of man: sustenance, deliverance from our sins, deliverance from evil.

First we must carefully analyse the exact meaning of each of the words used by Jesus in this part of the Our Father: 'daily, give us, today, bread, our'.

' Daily': necessary for today

Commentators have long struggled over this part of the Our Father, at first sight so simple and clear, because of difficulties over the Greek word epiúsion, which is traditionally rendered as 'daily'.

Amazingly, this Greek word is not found in any other text in the New Testament, nor anywhere else in the whole Greek Bible. In fact it was not ever used even in Greek secular literature. It has been found in a Greek ('koiné' or popular Greek) text dating from 500 years after the New Testament, but in the plural: its meaning there is 'provisions for the day' and it is actually followed by a shopping list.

The translation 'give us this day our daily bread' therefore involves an attempt to interpret this rare Greek word. The interpretation is faithful enough perhaps, but it might be amplified thus: 'give us this day the bread necessary for today'.

The present translation 'daily bread' goes back to the *Itala antica*, the oldest Latin translation of the Bible. Some experts translate the word 'daily' by the expression 'up till tomorrow', which gives the meaning: 'give us today the sustenance we need until tomorrow'. This translation has a clear Biblical reference to the Old Testament manna - which lasted just one day: there was no point storing it up because it did not keep. Thus the Greek text suggests that we should not allow ourselves to be preoccupied by petty calculations about the future.

'Bread': in a material or a metaphorical sense?

Another word on which the experts are divided is 'bread'. You might think that bread is ... bread, and yet we do frequently use it in a metaphorical sense. When we say 'to earn one's bread' we mean 'to look after oneself, to pay one's way'. In the Bible bread is often used in a metaphorical sense.

In the book of Genesis we find: 'By the sweat of your face will you earn your bread' (3:19). Here the reference is obviously to our general sustenance with everything necessary for life: home, food, and clothing.

On another occasion Jesus made the same point even more vividly: 'I am the living bread which has come down from heaven. Anyone who eats this bread will live for ever; and the bread that I shall give is my flesh, for the life of the world.' (*John* 6: 51). Here the bread is that of the Eucharist.

No wonder then that there have been debates among the experts as to how to interpret the sentence 'give us this day our daily bread'. But however we decide to interpret the word bread, one thing is quite certain: it needs to be taken in a physical, material sense, it needs to be understood in the broad sense of nourishment, of sustenance.

'Give us' : *the prayer of petition*

Since God is our Father, and fathers are interested in everything that is of interest to their children, he cares about our material needs too, but Jesus tells us very clearly elsewhere that material interests are not to dominate the interests of the spirit: "Set your hearts on his Kingdom first, and on God's saving justice, and all these other things will be given to you as well' So do not worry..." (*Matthew* 6:33).

Jesus says this for one very simple reason: that we are tempted to make material problems into very big problems, and spiritual problems into very small ones. Jesus himself had to cope with material problems (for thirty years he was a workman, he had to sweat and labour too), but he teaches us never to allow material problems to take away our peace nor to sacrifice the highest goods to material ones.

Jesus laid great emphasis on the prayer of petition: 'Ask, and it will be given to you ... knock and the door will be opened to you ... What father among you, if his son asked for a fish, would hand him a snake? Or if he asked for an egg, hand him a scorpion?' (*Luke* 11:9-12).

So we are to ask God for what we need: bread, fish, egg, work, health, reasonable success, peace, tranquility, a clear future, a good marriage, good and healthy children. Jesus teaches us to do this with all the simplicity and directness of a child.

If someone questions whether it can be right to leave to God problems that are really down to our own responsibility, the answer is clear: Jesus certainly doesn't teach us to sit on our backsides. Whole pages of the Gospel set out Christ's teaching on the subject: the parable of the talents clearly states that we ought to get busy with using all God's gifts. Woe betide the person who buries any one of them, for Christ is never on the side of the cowards, the exploiters, or the parasites.

On the other hand, everybody knows that there are huge problems about which we can do absolutely nothing. When we have done all we can without managing to solve such a problem, Christ tells us to present it to God in faith: 'everything you ask and pray for, believe that you have it already, and it will be yours.' (*Mark* 11:24).

But surely there will be problems that God will refuse to resolve? 'Ask in my name' says Jesus. What does this mean? It means something very profound, it means asking in union with him, united to his person, having all that we ask ratified by him. Christ's authorisation is very important, because in order to get it I must first ask myself if what I am asking for is in conformity with his will.

Christ then asks me to investigate the problem I am facing further, to investigate it in the light of the Gospel, with the Gospel in my hands. First, I have to ask myself this: is what I am wanting actually in accordance with the mind of Christ? Will Christ set his seal of authorisation on what I am asking for? If I can say 'yes', then I must boldly present the problem to God with complete certainty of being heard.

Jesus makes great promises about the granting of prayers prayed in faith, but he makes no promise as to the when. He does not say at any point in the gospel that the Father will respond to your problem immediately. Often God's slowness to respond matures my view of the problem - or matures the problem itself. God's answers almost always go way beyond our petitions, he gives us much, much more than we asked for, but sometimes he responds rather late in the day.

God's delays are important! They make our faith, our humility, and our generosity grow. They draw out the gifts that we had buried. They make us resourceful and active, they mature us. God's delays are often important in relation to what we ask for, and they often serve to render our petitions better.

'Today': asking day by day

All too often it happens that we fail to solve our problems. I may have a big spiritual problem - for example I want to be set free from a particular vice - and I present it to God in the name of Christ, and yet all too often God does not answer me.

One reason may be that I have failed to notice a very important aspect of the teaching of Christ: in our desire to embrace our future, we forget our present. In other words we often want to eliminate this or that very tricky problem with a prayer, bypassing logic and responsibility.

Jesus brings us back to the concrete reality of problems. In the tactic of 'praying for the day' about the problem of that day' he gives us a profoundly wise rule of life. He teaches us that the most difficult problems in our lives, when faced day by day, step by step, moment by moment, are resolvable. But if I try to resolve everything at a stroke, I won't settle anything.

This then is the tactic that Jesus teaches me to enable me to turn seemingly insurmountable problems into surmountable ones.

Do you have some addiction from which you just can't manage to break free? Are you a victim of drink, drugs, or the vice of impurity? Are you ashamed? Do you want to free yourself? Christ teaches us the way: 'Ask the Father in faith every day to break that chain of addiction'. You will break it! The Father hears you only when you are collaborating with him.

If you ask for 'a one-off' to eliminate the problem, God will almost certainly be deaf to your plea. He cannot. If you ask for 'a one-off', you almost certainly do not have the serious intention of collaborating with him. God cannot give you ready-made food; if he did, he would be a very poor father, because he would be encouraging you in your inertia.

If you ask for today, you will probably be collaborating with God, and God will rescue you if you do your part.

'Our': asking for others too

Christ wants us to be attentive to the problems of others. No person who is totally absorbed in his own problems can be considered a Christian. The problems of those who are close to me, the person who is entrusted to me, the person who has a connection with me, are to be especially close to my heart. Nor should I be oblivious to others' suffering and heartaches even when I have no personal connection with them.

Any Christian who sees that someone else has a problem must open himself to that problem. A Christian wearing blinkers so as not to see other people's needs is simply not conceivable for Christ. In thinking about the problems of others I am also taking care of my own, since God cannot fail to give a helping hand to the person who has a generous heart for others.

Forgive us our Trespasses

Matthew writes 'Forgive us our debts' whereas Luke writes 'Forgive us our sins', explaining that our sins put us in debt to God. The clarification is interesting.

For purposes of precision, Luke uses a Greek term that conveys the idea of 'a mistake', it is a term that archers used when they missed the target; the idea was that of 'a miss'. Strange that if someone pulls off a successful piece of trickery the Christian says 'he has committed a sin', the non-Christian thinks 'bullseye!', but God answers 'No! it's a miss!'.

The word 'debt' calls for more thought. If sin is a debt contracted to God, this means that our life belongs to God, our actions belong to him, we cannot consider ourselves the exclusive masters of our actions. We were created by him, we must live for him, we must act for him. To sin is to betray God, to defraud God, to rob him of something.

We have so many debts to God! Origen wrote very boldly: 'No living man spends an hour of the day or of the night without contracting a debt'. He was probably alluding to our debts of gratitude towards God, for our sins are real debts because they manifest our real ingratitude in the face of his love. This ingratitude covers us from head to foot, it accompanies us like our shadow.

The equivalent to Matthew's expression 'as we forgive those who are indebted to us' in Luke is 'since we too have forgiven'. The meaning is broadly speaking the same, Matthew links the request for forgiveness to a formal commitment to forgive, while in Luke the request for forgiveness is reinforced by the assumption that we ourselves have already forgiven.

But Christ's idea is clear: 'when you stand in prayer, forgive whatever you have against anybody, so that your Father in heaven may forgive your failings too.' (*Mark* 11:25).

God forgives us

If Jesus calls us to ask him for it, then forgiveness is a real possibility - and no gift is as great as this one! The weight of sin on our shoulders is heavy indeed, and the need for peace is real and profound. When we have peace we are profoundly happy, even with a multitude of crosses.

But does God forgive any and every sin? How can we be absolutely sure that our sins have been forgiven by God? These are key questions.

Yes, God forgives us our sins, he forgives any sin, however serious, provided that our hearts are detached from evil, provided that we have sincerity, truth, and good will, provided that we are also good to others.

The totality of the conditions we have just enumerated is what the theologians have called 'penitence'. If someone is penitent, God forgives that person now, he forgives him completely. Jesus did it so many times in his earthly life, and he also taught it with crystal clarity.

He said to the paralytic 'My child, your sins are forgiven.' (*Mark* 2:5). The sick man asked for healing, he gave him healing of body and of soul. Why did he do it? Jesus saw a great faith in this poor man, who had had himself lowered with ropes in front of him. What is great faith if not great will?

Zacchaeus the profiteer, the cheat, was forgiven by Christ, who said goodbye to him with the words 'Today salvation has come to this house'. The thing that determined Jesus to forgive him was his penitence. Zacchaeus expressed his penitence in the words 'Look sir, I am going to give half my property to the poor, and if I have cheated anybody I will pay him back four times the amount.' (*Luke* 19:8-9).

To the good thief on the cross who cried out to Christ 'Jesus, remember me when you come into your kingdom', Jesus replied immediately: 'I tell you, today you will be with me in paradise' Why did he forgive him? Because he saw the sincerity in this poor wretch: 'In our case we deserved it' (*Luke* 23: 41-41).

Forgiveness of sins is assured

The first stage in the recognition of sin is penitence. We have the solemn word of that this will unquestionably lead to forgiveness.

Here is a very strong statement: 'It is not the healthy who need the doctor, but the sick... I came to call not the upright, but sinners.' (*Matthew* 9:13). 'There will be more rejoicing in heaven over one sinner repenting than over ninety-nine upright people who have no need of repentance.' (*Luke*

15:7). In other words, if there is penitence, there is immediate forgiveness.

But Christ wanted to do even more, he wanted to give the penitent sinner an absolute security. He conferred on the Church the power to forgive sins: 'Receive the Holy Spirit. If you forgive anyone's sins, they are forgiven; if you retain anyone's sins, they are retained.' (*John* 20:22). This is how the sacrament of forgiveness was born in the Church, the sacrament of reconciliation, the sacrament of peace and joy! It is an act of tenderness on the part of the risen Christ towards us, the first gift of the risen Christ to make it possible for us to rise from all sadness.

How can we be absolutely sure we are penitent? It was to answer this very need that God established a human judge, the Church, to give security and peace! Hence the origins of the sacrament of reconciliation, to guarantee peace of heart to us all on the basis of the Church's confirmation.

So often people ask why the forgiveness of God has to be given through the forgiveness of the priest, but the answer is simple! Each one of our sins is more than a debt contracted to God, it is in addition a debt contracted to our fellows. So it was that Christ ordained that if we wanted God's forgiveness we must first ask for forgiveness from our fellows. The ordinary priest before whom I kneel represents my fellows to me: when he - i.e. my fellows - has forgiven me, then God too forgives me.

We too must forgive

Jesus tells us this very clearly, and moreover he practised it himself repeatedly and insistently.

Forgive us as we forgive others. If we had composed the Our Father ourselves, we would probably have put it like this: 'Father, forgive our our sins, even if we don't always manage to forgive others'. That isn't the way Jesus looks at it. He doesn't mince his words, there's no compromise you must forgive whatever the cost!

One day Peter thought he could show off by going one better than the Jewish practice of forgiving up to three times: he said he was ready to forgive up to 'seven times'. Jesus replied: 'Not seven, I tell you, but seventy-seven times' (*Matthew* 18:22).

After recording the words of the Our Father, Matthew adds: 'if you forgive others their failings, your heavenly Father will forgive you yours; but if you do not forgive others, your Father will not forgive your failings either.' (*Matthew* 6:14).

So we have to forgive generously - but how to do it when forgiveness is so difficult? When the person who has hurt me is completely in the wrong? When resentment destroys my peace of mind and rankles like poison? Here are some suggestions.

1. Every time you find yourself dwelling on the wrong you have suffered, call down God's blessings wholeheartedly on the person who has injured you. This is a deeply healing prayer that will give you peace, it is the forgiveness of God that comes down on others and on ourselves.

2. Don't ever let yourself mention by name in conversation the person who has injured you. The tactic of silence is crucial! Even if the whole world is talking about that person, you, who could say so much, should be generous enough to stay silent. This is another kind of forgiveness, one that is very precious, it purifies you and helps you to grow into a big-hearted and generous person.

Lead us not into Temptation

This part of the Our Father may sound strange, and it is easily misunderstood. Are we really meant to ask God not to be tempted?

Actually the traditional wording here is not a very happy rendering of the Greek text, which was translated too literally into Latin, and then into English at this point. Translators can all too easily become traducers!

A couple of verses in the letter of James provide an excellent commentary on this part of the Our Father. 'Never, when you are being put to the test, say 'God is tempting me': God cannot be tempted by evil, and he does not put anybody to the test. Everyone is put to the test by being attracted and seduced by that person's own wrong desire' (*James* 1:13-14).

Temptation, struggle, test

First, we need to bear in mind that the Greek word *peirasmós* rendered here by 'temptation' has more than one meaning. 'Temptation' and 'struggle' to begin with - but the word 'to tempt' itself, in addition to the obvious meaning, may also signify 'to test' or 'to assay' or, in modern parlance, 'to take a test'.

For example, St Paul says these strange words: 'Put yourselves to the test to make sure you are in the faith' (*2 Corinthians* 13:5).

Another way of putting this would be 'Examine yourselves to see if you are in the faith', i.e. 'take a test'.

So the word 'temptation' can have these three meanings: first, 'temptation' pure and simple, second 'struggle', third 'test'. It can mean 'testing', 'assaying', 'taking a test'.

A precise explanation of this clause in the Our Father cannot then start from the word 'temptation', since it is too ambiguous. We must pay attention to the context.

The context tells us that this is a petition for salvation, as we can see when we read it in parallel with the following clause, which calls for salvation from the evil one: 'lead us not into temptation/but deliver us from Evil'.

The prayer 'lead us not into temptation' can therefore be explained in this way: 'do not leave us when we are being tested, do not abandon us when you are testing us, come to the aid of our weakness when you are testing us'.

Testing is necessary

We should not be surprised when God puts us to the test, we should not be surprised when we have to struggle. It would be amazing if there were no struggle, for life was given to us to struggle through, not to sleep through. Life is about struggle, it is not about growing up wrapped in cotton wool. It's only when we have to struggle that our personality begins to develop. To struggle is to love, to conquer evil is to love, to conquer our pettiness is to love, we only really know how to love God when we have struggled to love Him.

Call it struggle or call it temptation, the first rule is not to be surprised when we experience it. The second rule is not to play with temptation or to flirt with danger: 'The spirit is willing' - warned Christ - 'but the flesh is weak'. You have very powerful desires but your weakness is far greater than you can imagine.

But we do have a guarantee that we will always be able to cope with temptation: Christ told us exactly what to do: 'Stay awake, and pray not to be put to the test.' (*Matthew* 26:41).

Prayer is the secret

There is no problem that cannot be resolved by prayer. There is no temptation, struggle, or test that cannot be overcome with prayer.

Look to God and ask for the miracle of being freed from evil. Keep on asking for it every day, for you will not eliminate the problem 'at a stroke'. This hammering at the heart of God is important, it opens you up to faith. God can get to work on you only when you open yourself up to faith, when you really grasp your need for him, and then figure out your own role.

Deliver us from Evil

The final petition in the Our Father is simply the extension of 'lead us not into temptation', and needs to be read together with it to be properly understood.

The Greek text has a much more forceful ring than the English translation. A better rendering of the sense of the original would be 'tear us away' instead of 'deliver us'. We ask God to defend us and liberate us by his power from the powerful and invasive pressure of evil, and we beg for salvation from it.

The original Greek speaks of 'the Evil one', it is a masculine adjective, a personification. The expression 'the Evil One' is common in the New Testament with reference to Satan. In the parable of the darnel Jesus explains that the darnel sown on top of the good grain to stifle it is the work of the Evil One: 'the enemy who sowed it, the Evil One.' (*Matthew* 13:39). And John: 'I have written to you, young people, because you are strong, and God's word remains in you, and you have overcome the Evil One.' (*1 John* 2:14).

A mysterious force called evil

In the New Testament we find various names for the Evil One: Satan, Devil, Demon. The word Satan is a common name, it means 'the enemy', and derives from the Hebrew verb 'satan', 'to be an enemy'. But the word 'Devil' is an adjective, it means 'accuser'; it derives from the Greek word 'diaballo', which means 'to accuse, to calumniate'. 'Demon' is also a Greek word, it originally meant 'power of the beyond'.

This term 'the Evil One' as used here in the Our Father can be understood as implying the personification of evil. There is in the world a mysterious force that is called evil, everyone knows it, it is an overwhelming suffocating force. But in the Our Father, Christ taught us not to be afraid of evil because he has conquered it for ever.

The force of evil surrounds us, camouflaging itself, threatening us, but Christ is telling us that we have the resources to face up to it. Those resources are vigilance and prayer: 'Stay awake, and pray not to be put to the test.' (*Matthew* 26:41).

Christ knows our weakness and our naïveté. We are thoughtless children who rush lightheartedly to gather flowers without noticing the serpent lurking in the middle of them. Making us pray repeatedly to resolve the problem of evil, Jesus wants us to be on our guard against carelessness. It is vital that we become aware of our weakness, that we become aware of how much we need him.

Manifestations of Satan

There are so many manifestations of Satan today, we need to dwell on them for a moment.

The first of these manifestations is the widespread ignorance about religion. Satan is delighted at the sight of so many ignorant people. He can do whatever he likes with the ignorant, he can make them swallow anything. The way to defend ourselves is obvious, we have to get ourselves properly educated. We have to look for the right sort of books, we have to dig deep into the Word of God. It's also a very good thing to get involved in teaching. Give a hand with catechesis, and you will find that in teaching children you will be learning yourself.

The other maninfestation of Satan is the sophisticated lie, lying turned into a system. The lies of the mass media - where Satan rules through falsehood, pornography, a schooling in hedonism and violence. We all absorb it, we are all poisoned by it. We must react, we must denounce and boycott, we must also be creative. Do what you can.

A third tremendous manifestation of Satan is widespread pessimism. Satan knows how to pollute everything with pessimism, but the Christian cannot be a pessimist, for he knows that Christ has conquered the world, he is the ruler of history, he is the victor over the future. Open your eyes and see the immensity of the good achieved by Christians in the world! Where is Christ not present in his witnesses, witnesses ready to sacrifice even their lives for his cause?

In the time of Christ there were people who were possessed. They are still around today, only now they are called 'addicts', people addicted to violence, drugs, drink, sex.

The possessed were a cause of suffering to Christ, and he liberated them. What are we to do with the possessed in today's world? Exactly the same as what Jesus Christ did - treat them with infinite compassion and bring them the power of God. A possessed person cannot be liberated by words, he needs Christ. We have to give Christ to them.

Should we be discouraged because there are so many addicts, alcoholics, sex-addicts, criminals around us today? No. Christ came for them, he wants to heal them, he loves them with infinite tenderness. He wants to heal them, but he wants to do it for them through us.

Here then is a plan of action for all of us. When we get to work on it, we shall be contributing our part to the final petition in the Our Father: 'Deliver us from evil'.

Informative Catholic Reading

We hope that you have enjoyed reading this booklet.

If you would like to find out more about CTS booklets - we'll send you our free information pack and catalogue.

Please send us your details:

   Name ....
   Address ....
   ....
   ....
   Postcode ....
   Telephone...
   Email ....

Send to: CTS, 40-46 Harleyford Road,
           Vauxhall, London
           SE11 5AY

Tel: 020 7640 0042
Fax: 020 7640 0046
Email: info@cts-online.org.uk